Celtic Fashions

Tom Tierney

DOVER PUBLICATIONS, INC.
Mineola, New York

INTRODUCTION

The Celts (generally pronounced with a hard *c,* but also with a soft *c*) were less a race than a tribal, nomadic culture held together by family ties and common language. The earliest-known major Celtic settlement, located near the Upper Danube, dates from about 800 B.C. Some historians believe that the "sacred stone" communities of Britain's Stonehenge and Ireland's Newgrange of 5,000 years ago were of Celtic origin. By 300 B.C., Celtic strongholds extended from Romania and Hungary to France and Spain, continuing across the sea to England, Ireland, Scotland, and Wales. These territories were called *Celtica* by the ancient Greeks; the people were called *Keltoi* and *Galatae.* Later, the Romans referred to the people as *Celtae* or *Galli.*

Centuries before the founding of the Roman Empire, the Celts were trading with Greeks and Etruscans. The Celts created the first distinctive style of art in continental Europe, as well as introducing iron and bronze technology, including innovations such as the plowshare, horseshoe, reaping machine, rotary flour mill, spoked iron-rimmed wheel, two-edged sword, and chain mail. Celtic metal workers were noted for their artistry and craftsmanship in the design of swords, body armor, helmets, and shields, as well as in metal cauldrons, drinking cups, mirrors, bracelets, necklaces, and brooches. Consistent design elements used in Celtic art are elaborate intertwined geometric shapes, which have been found in many archaeological sites; the earliest known motif is the double-spiral found on stone carvings and jewelry.

As the Celts became more technologically proficient and developed their farming and trade, a wealthy ruling class evolved. Tribal chieftains extended their influence in the form of feudalism.

Published in Canada by General Publishing Company, Ltd., 895 Don Mills Road, 400-2 Park Centre, Toronto, Ontario M3C 1W3.
Published in the United Kingdom by David & Charles, Brunel House, Forde Close, Newton Abbot, Devon TQ12 4PU.

Bibliographical Note

Celtic Fashions is a new work, first published by Dover Publications, Inc., in 2002.

DOVER *Pictorial Archive* SERIES

This book belongs to the Dover Pictorial Archive Series. You may use the designs and illustrations for graphics and crafts applications, free and without special permission, provided that you include no more than four in the same publication or project. (For permission for additional use, please write to Permissions Department, Dover Publications, Inc., 31 East 2nd Street, Mineola, N.Y. 11501.)
However, republication or reproduction of any illustration by any other graphic service, whether it be in a book or in any other design resource, is strictly prohibited.

International Standard Book Number: 0-486-42075-2

Manufactured in the United States of America
Dover Publications, Inc., 31 East 2nd Street, Mineola, N.Y. 11501

The Celts, however, never were able to unify into a single powerful nation or empire, as did the Romans. Celtic women shared equal rights with men, continuing to own property after marriage; they often fought alongside men in battle, with some women ruling as chieftains of their tribal groups. By 400 B.C., Celtic leaders were generally selected by a type of consensus, rather than by inheritance. Celts were established in Spain by the fifth century B.C. In 390 B.C., they sacked Rome; in 279 B.C., they invaded Greece and pillaged Delphi. However, the Gallic Celts were subjugated by the Romans in the first century B.C. Only in Ireland did the Celtic culture remain intact, surviving long after the Roman Empire had fallen.

During the sixth to eighth centuries, Celtic Ireland assumed an important role in the spread of Christianity, carrying the Celtic version to Britain, Wales, France, northern Italy, Austria, Germany, and Switzerland. There is evidence that the Celts believed in life after death, burying their dead with artifacts such as food, garments, and weapons. Aristocrats might be buried with gold and amber jewelry, and some were entombed in their carriages. A number of Celtic gods appear to date back to prehistoric times and even suggest ties with Asian deities. A principal Celtic holiday was Samhain [*sow in*, rhyming with *cow in*], a forerunner of Halloween that marked the final harvest or end of summer.

As there was no Celtic written language, information about Celtic religion has been gathered from reports by their enemies, the Romans. The ancient Celtic priests were called Druids; they served not only as religious leaders, but also as judges and arbitrators. These learned men—teachers, healers, poets, and mystics—were greatly admired by their society. By A.D. 100, most Druids had converted to Christianity, becoming priests, although many still clung to the old ways and thus began to be associated with wizardry and witchcraft. Merlin of King Arthur's court exemplifies this transitional Druid.

The Celts' principal form of entertainment was the banquet, a raucous event that might last for days. Typical foods were boiled pork and beef; fish; wild game such as venison, boar, wild cattle and fowl, and bear; bread; and cheese, honey, and butter. Imported wine was reserved for the wealthy; commoners drank beer and mead, a drink made from wheat or barley and honey.

The Celts bred hunting dogs, which they also used in battle. Horses were so important to the Celtic way of life that there was a goddess, Epona, who was the deity of the hunt and the horse [page 28]. In England, she was called Riannon; in Ireland, Macha. The largest representation of a horse in history is located at the site of a Celtic fort in Uffington, England. This 350-foot-long image was carved into a chalk hillside; it can be seen from twenty miles away. Today's sport of fox hunting harks back to the Celtic custom of hunting boar on horseback.

There are written accounts of early Celts going into battle unclothed, perhaps for religious reasons. However, ordinary Celtic warriors generally dressed for battle in *braccae* (breeches or trousers), tunics, and colorful cloaks. They also used body armor and chain mail, as well as bronze helmets, and they carried wood or leather shields worked with bronze. Their weapons included the long sword, spears, lances, javelins, and slings and bows. The leaders generally rode chariots into battle. By the time of Roman domination in the first centuries A.D. and B.C., there was little difference between the dress of the Gauls and the Irish Celts. Both men and women wore belted tunics with a cloak fastened by a *fibula* (clasp or brooch). Tunics and cloaks could be of many different colors, the cloaks' design frequently indicating social status. Brightly colored hooded Celtic cloaks became internationally popular among the rich, especially in Rome. By the fifth century A.D., Rome had fallen to the Goths and was no longer a force in England or Ireland. As the Romans withdrew, Ireland was invaded by Germanic tribes (principally Angles, Saxons, and Jutes), and many of the Romanized Celts fled to Wales, Cornwall, and Brittany, forming the "Celtic fringe" that persists to this day. It was during this period that King Arthur, a Celtic ruler fighting Saxon invaders, lived, although little factual material is known about him. In the eighth and ninth centuries, the Vikings (Norsemen) invaded Celtic Ireland, plundering it for many years. Eventually the Irish prevailed, and new arrivals from the overpopulated northern lands settled peacefully, becoming assimilated with the Celtic Irish.

The last invasion of Celtic Ireland came in the twelfth century from Normandy, land of William the Conqueror, who dominated Britain in the eleventh century. Since most Normans were of Celtic heritage, it was now a case of Celts invading Celts. It was from this point on that England began its 800-year power struggle to gain control over Ireland. The last great Celtic migration, in a sense, was the outflow of immigrants to North America.

Northern European Bronze Age Celts, ca. 2,000 B.C.

The Celtic penchant for jewelry is amply demonstrated here. Celts loved gold and worked with amber, jet, amethyst, and other colorful stones. **Left:** The man wears a knee-length belted garment and cloak fastened by a fibula.

Right: The woman is dressed in a long tunic and a shirt. He wears a sword, she carries a dagger. Both wear broad, patterned waistbands. The spiral motif in their jewelry possibly had a religious as well as a decorative function.

Late Bronze Age Teutonic Celts, ca. 1,000 B.C.

Left: This Teutonic-Celtic woman wears a long, sleeveless, belted tunic and carries a shawl. Across her chest is a decorative bandolier of leather with applied metallic geometric designs. **Right:** The man wears a hip-length beltless tunic over short Celtic *braccae* (breeches) with a shawl or cape. Early Celts enjoyed using bold, colorful stripes and checks in their woven fabrics. Both Celts wear an early form of *ghillies*—flexible moccasinlike shoes made of animal hide that were shaped to the foot by a drawstring. Shoes were made frequently because they did not have a separate sole of hardened leather. (See page 48 for a pattern of this type of shoe.)

Teutonic Celts, ca. 800 B.C.

Left: The man wears a long, belted tunic with elbow-length sleeves. He wears a torque (or *torc*) around his neck. The torque was a sacred neck ornament made of metal, either gold or a metal alloy. It appeared on figures of Celtic gods, giving it its sacred meaning; it also may have been a sign of the Celt's status or nobility. **Right:** The woman wears a short tunic over a long skirt. Her soft leather belt has a long fringe hanging from its bottom edge. Both wear "sunflower"-shaped decorative bronze belt buckles.

Teutonic Celts, ca. 800 B.C.

Left: The woman's long-sleeved tunic seems almost modern in its streamlined design; it is enhanced by a metal collar with raised geometric designs, as well as a belt with a large metal sunflower disk belt. **Right:** He wears a short, belted soft leather tunic under a knee-length wool cape pinned with a gold fibula. Under his leather-strip sandals he wears short knit stockings. Her hair is worn with a coarse fishnet-type snood; he wears a wool or felt cap.

Early Irish Celts, ca. 750 B.C.

Many Celts who lived in wooded, non-agricultural areas dressed in furs and skins, the products of their hunting way of life. **Left:** The man's tunic and cape are made of fur; he wears a leather bodice over a cloth shirt.

Right: The woman is dressed in a fur cloak and carries a helmet and spear, indicating that she is a skilled hunter. He wears an arm torque; she wears a neck torque.

Frankish Celts, ca. 450 B.C.

The Franks were a Germanic tribe who migrated to France—giving it their name—and eventually dominating that territory. The Germanic influence is seen in this family's costume: the woman's belted over-tunic, the man's short patterned pullover tunic, and the child's and man's leather-thong-wrapped leggings. The Celtic influences appear in the jewelry, weapons, and use of chain mail.

European Celts, ca. 400 B.C.

The Celts were nomadic, continually moving on. The causes could have been defeat by an enemy, the search for richer lands, or possibly an exploding population. **Left:** The man wears a heavy wool cloak over a woolen tunic. **Center:** The woman wears a hooded cloak over a long plaid woolen tunic and carries her child, who wears a tunic and has a shawl. **Right:** The boy wears a hooded cloak over a tunic and *braccae*. Both man and boy wear leggings of sheepskin, bound with leather thongs.

European-Celtic chieftain and warrior, ca. 400 B.C.

These men belong to the same nomadic tribe as the Celts shown on the previous page. **Left:** The chieftain wears a fur outer tunic and leggings over a wool tunic and trousers. **Right:** The warrior wears coarse-textured woolen breeches, a wool tunic, and a long cloak. He carries a wooden shield.

European Celts, ca. 300 B.C.

Left: The farmer wears a wool tunic with bold checks over long breeches that are gathered at the ankles. He is greeting a neighboring chieftain, who rides in a wicker-and-wood cart with his wife and son. **Right:** The chieftain is dressed in the same manner as the farmer, except that he wears a gold torque around his neck. The woman wears a long-sleeved belted tunic and a shawl, the boy a belted tunic.

Gallic Celts, ca. 300 B.C.

These Gallic Celts are shown in a metalwork workshop. **Left:** The woman wears a short-sleeved, belted plaid wool tunic. She is admiring a bronze mirror. **Center:** The man wears a short-sleeved tunic over plaid wool braccae.

Right: The metalsmith wears an apron of soft leather. In Celtic society, the smith had almost supernatural status and was considered as much a sorcerer as a craftsman.

13

Gallic Celts, ca. 200 B.C.

Left: The man is dressed in a sleeveless rope-belted tunic and wears gold bracelets, leg bands, and necklaces. He wears his hair in ponytails. **Right:** The woman wears a loose, full-sleeved tunic over a straight skirt. She wears her blonde hair in a loose, flowing style.

British-Celtic warriors, ca. 150 B.C.

Two of the warriors shown above are unclothed except for foot covering, helmets, weapons, and shields. One warrior, probably a farmer who has joined in the battle, wears plaid braccae and shoes. He brandishes a spear decorated with a skull. The Celts often cut off the heads of their enemies and displayed the skulls as prized trophies. The man with the helmet is probably the chieftain; his helmet has horns representing the ox, an animal sacred to the Celts. He also wears a golden torque around his neck.

Gallic-Celtic warriors, ca. 100 B.C.

Left: He wears wool braccae, as well as a *sagum*—a cape or cloak made of a folded rectangle of wool, pinned by a thorn; when opened out it was used as a blanket. He wears a horned helmet and carries a single-edged sword, which probably meant that he was a mercenary hired by the Romans. **Right:** This warrior wears a striped long-sleeved wool tunic with a broad attached collar-cape and braccae. On his head he wears a cap of long fur; around his neck is an embossed bronze gorget and gold necklace. The long horn that he holds in his right hand is shaped like an animal head; he also holds a shield of wood and boiled leather and wears a sword.

Southern British-Celtic farm women, ca. 100 B.C.

These women are preparing a meal. **Left:** She carries a basket of vegetables and wears a long-sleeved belted tunic of brightly colored wool plaid. **Right:** This woman is gathering grain that has been stored in a pit dug in the ground. These pits were covered with wicker lids, and when they were emptied, scraps and bones and other waste were thrown in and then covered with dirt. She wears a shirt and belted skirt of different plaid patterns. The Celts loved and used bright colors in their fabrics.

Celtic common folk, ca. 49 B.C.

By the time of the Roman conquest of the Gauls and occupation of the British Isles, there was little difference between the dress of the English and the Gallic Celts.

The common folk generally wore plaid woolen tunics, and braccae or skirts.

Queen Boudicca, ca. A.D. 60

The Celtic-English queen Boudicca (or Boudica) led an uprising against the Roman occupiers of her homeland in A.D. 60. This legendary figure was described as having either golden or red hair and wearing a brightly colored cloak or tunic. She wore a heavy gold torque when riding her chariot in battle. Celtic women were known for their courage, but Queen Boudicca was one of the few known to have borne weapons. She won several battles, but Roman soldiers finally defeated her army.

19

Celtic Druids, ca. A.D. 100

Druids were keepers of tradition, history, and law among their tribes. The Irish or English Druids held their religious ceremonies in wooded glades, where they made offerings to the gods by casting donated jewelry or other prized possessions into sacred springs or streams. According to Roman reports, the Druids dressed in long white robes. There also are some accounts of female Druids dressed in black.

Gallic-Celtic warriors, ca. A.D. 100

The early Celts often were employed as mercenaries by the Roman army. **Left:** This man is a foot soldier who uses a slingshot. He wears braccae and a cloak fastened by a fibula. **Right:** This warrior wears a Roman version of battle attire—chest armor worn over a tunic—although he still wears the Celtic hair and beard styles, as well as a torque about his neck.

Teutonic-Celtic chieftain and warrior, ca. A.D. 100

Left: The chieftain wears plaid braccae under a long tunic that is caught up at the waist; his cloak is pinned over his shoulders with a fibula. His plaid wool cap is twisted into a knot at the side. **Right:** The warrior wears closely fitted braccae made of horizontal strips of material. A plaid shawl is draped over his neck and shoulders. He leans on a battle ax. His long hair is pulled to the side in a distinctive "twist."

Celtic commoners, ca. A.D. 100

By the second century, the Celts were firmly entrenched in Britain and Ireland. These two farmers are representative of the common folk. Both wear belted tunics. In addition, the man on the left has a short plaid scarf thrown over his shoulders; the man on the right wears his scarf like a cape, held together by a sunflower-motif fibula. He wears a hood and wool leggings held in place by soft leather straps.

Irish Celts, ca. A.D. 150

Both the man and the woman wear their hair in the typical long-flowing Celtic manner. **Left:** The man wears a wool cloak draped over his shoulders. **Center:** The boy wears a belted tunic and braccae. **Right:** The woman wears a belted Roman-style toga draped over one shoulder.

Saint Patrick, A.D. 432

Saint Patrick was a British Celt who was kidnapped and taken to Ireland at the age of sixteen. He worked there until he escaped and traveled to France to become a priest. He then returned to Ireland, bringing Christianity in A.D. 432. His costume is based on an illustration from the Book of Kells, the early-ninth-century illuminated manuscript comprised of the four gospels. The Christian convert next to him wears a belted gown under a long cloak edged in an abstract design. Saint Patrick and his followers initiated the "golden age" of Irish learning.

Celtic warriors, ca. A.D. 500

By A.D. 407, Rome had withdrawn its troops from Britain and Ireland, leaving these regions vulnerable to invasions by groups such as Saxons, Picts, and Vikings. Around this time, King Arthur, the fabled British-Celtic ruler, became a hero for his stand against the pagan Saxons and other Germanic invaders. This woman and man are both Celtic warriors from this period. **Left:** The woman wears a belted woolen tunic in colorful checks over braccae. **Right:** The man wears braccae and neck and arm torques; his torso and arms are profusely decorated with tattoos.

The Celtic god Cernunnos

One of the oldest of the Celtic gods was Cernunnos [*ker noo nohs*], the Stag god. He was depicted with the antlers of a stag, holding a torque in one hand and a snake with a ram's head in the other. The shirt and braccae are based on a pre-historic sculpture, so it is not known whether the costume consisted of striped fabric or possibly animal skins that were pieced together. Some speculate that the Christian depiction of Satan is based on the image of Cernunnos.

The Celtic goddess Epona

Epona was the Celtic goddess of fertility and animal husbandry. She was usually shown riding a horse sidesaddle while carrying a bird. In this representation she is shown in medieval attire, although her origins go back to pre-historic times. There were many Celtic gods, known only through representations on artifacts or through Roman historical accounts, but little is known of each god's position in the Celtic pantheon.

Arthurian period British-Celtic warriors, ca. A.D. 500

Both warriors wear leather and metal body armor over braccae; they wear metal helmets. The warrior on the left has fur-lined leggings and carries a battle ax.

British-Celtic chieftain and soldier, ca. A.D. 500

These men were the prototypes for the Arthurian knights in armor. It is interesting to note that most movie depictions of King Arthur and his court show the knights dressed in thirteenth and fourteenth century costume, because that was when most of the tales were recorded. **Left:** The warrior wears tunic-style chain mail. **Right:** The soldier is dressed in a kilt-type garment and a long shawl, both in a large check.

Arthurian period British Celts, ca. A.D. 500

This well-dressed couple are representative of the land-owning nobility class. **Left:** The woman wears a gown with a fitted bodice; the gown is trimmed with fur and has a decorative border. **Right:** The man wears a sleeve-less belted tunic of woolen plaid over shaggy-textured wool breeches. His arms are tattooed; around his neck he wears a gold torque. His cape is fastened with a large fibula.

British-Celtic women and child, ca. A.D. 600

These women of the late Arthurian period are shown performing home crafts—cording, spinning, and weaving. The costumes worn by the seated women have fitted bodices in the medieval style. The woman who is standing while working at the loom wears a shirt and skirt in colorful plaids. The child is wrapped in a plaid scarf.

Finn Mac Cool, ca. A.D. 600

One of the earliest of the fabled British-Celtic heroes was Finn Mac Cool, whose tale dates from the third century. Many of his adventures were later attributed to King Arthur. Mac Cool is shown in the medieval dress of the twelfth century, the period when his stories were first set down. He wears a cape over a belted tunic over leggings with leather ties. His companion wears a flowing gown beneath a cloak.

Cuchulainn, ca. A.D. 600

Cuchulainn [among the various Celtic pronunciations are *koo* **hool** *in, koo* **kool** *in,* or *koo* **chull** *in*] was another British-Celtic hero. He was the son of the god Lugh [*loo*]. In his legendary adventure, Cuchulainn was pitted against Queen Maeve [*mayv*] in a struggle for possession

of a magic bull. He is shown above in the garb of a hunter, wearing a fur stole over a short belted tunic that allows freedom of movement. His wool hose are bound by leather ties; he wears tie-on leather shoes.

Twelfth-century British-Celtic woman

She wears a medieval-style belted gown with flowing bell sleeves and a matching stole. The gown incorporates plaid fabric and elaborate embroidered motifs with an overskirt embellished with plaid edging and embroidery. The sleeves have plaid lining with insets of brightly colored triangles. There were restrictions on the use of color: for example, the higher the rank of the wearer, the more colors could be used in his or her costume. Only kings could wear as many as seven colors in a single costume.

Sixteenth-century Scottish Celts

About the ninth century, Irish Celts had migrated to the highlands of Scotland, eventually mixing with the native Picts. After A.D. 842, the Pict culture had virtually disappeared. Shown above are sixteenth-century Scottish Celts in highland dress. **Left:** The man wears a cloth shirt with an early form of the kilt, belted and with a matching bodice.

Attached to the belt is a sporran [purse] and dagger. **Center:** The lady wears a blouse with deep military cuffs on the sleeve, a short front-opening overskirt, an ankle-length wool petticoat, and a wool cape pinned with a large brooch. **Right:** The boy wears a short jacket over a wool kilt. The Scottish Celts are barefoot, in typical highland fashion.

Sixteenth-century Irish Celts

Under King Henry VIII, the English began giving land grants to English nobility in Ireland, driving the native Irish Celts off their lands and forcing them onto less arable soil. Most were reduced to poverty and became known as Wilde Irish. The struggle between England and Ireland over the control of the island dates from that time. **Left:** The woman is wearing a fur-trimmed hat with ear flaps; over her skirt she wears a cloak with scalloped edging. **Right:** Over his tunic, the boy wears a shirt with sleeves consisting of multicolored bands. He plays the bagpipes, a musical instrument associated with Scotland but having a long history; bagpipes were used in ancient Egypt as well as the Roman Empire.

Sixteenth-century Irish-Celtic "Wilde Irish"

Left: He wears a helmet and bits and pieces of English military attire (probably taken from English soldiers slain in skirmishes) over his short tunic and carries a pike or spear. **Right:** This Irish Celt is dressed similarly but wears a long sword in a sheath as well as a dagger on his belt. He carries a scabbard slung over his shoulder, which he probably uses in lieu of a sporran pouch.

Seventeenth-century Irish Celts

By the seventeenth century, some Irish Celts had moved up the social ladder and were intermingling with the English. They adopted the English styles, as seen here, although they retained some of their Celtic ways, such as their preference for bright colors and elaborate jewelry. **Left:** She wears a fur-lined cape fastened with a large fibula and a standing ruff. **Right:** He also wears a fur-lined cape, with knee breeches and slip-on shoes.

Eighteenth-century Scottish Highlander Celts

An eighteenth-century Scottish Highlander is shown with the young woman he is courting, as well as her mother. **Left:** He wears a jacket, kilt, cape, and *trews* (fitted trousers), all done in the same plaid. **Center:** The mother has pulled a stole over her head to form a hood. **Right:** The young lady wears a bodice, sleeves, overskirt, and stole of matching plaid over a plain white petticoat. During the 1700s, the English banned the wearing of plaids and family tartans, even arresting people who wore them on the street. Many Scots who migrated to America at that time proudly brought their plaids with them as an act of defiance.

Late-eighteenth-century Irish Celts

By this time most Irish dress was based on international styles; however, due to the country's poverty, the used-clothing business was the principal industry. Most common folk patched their threadbare garments. **Left:** The older woman wears the sturdy garments of the fisher folk; she probably made them herself. **Center:** The man's outfit probably is store-bought. **Right:** His lady has made her own and her baby's garments. Weaving and sewing were essential cottage industries in Ireland.

41

Early-nineteenth-century Irish-Celtic fisher folk

Left: The fishwife wears a cloak with a voluminous hood; the Irish cloak was a weatherproof garment of napped broadcloth that was expected to last a lifetime. Under her hood she wears a starched linen cap. She wears a white cotton blouse over her skirt, as well as an apron of striped broadcloth folded over at the waist for extra protection against the elements. **Right:** The fisherman wears a short jacket over a vest and a cable-knit sweater. He has high-topped oilskin boots and wears a tarred hat.

Late-nineteenth-century Irish-Celtic step dancers

Left: The dancer wears a modestly bustled dress of colorful wool with embroidered Celtic designs on the skirt. A *brat* (short cape) hangs from the collar of her dress.
Right: This dancer wears a "Dolly Varden" ensemble with side puffs [*panniers*] over a bell-shaped skirt, frilled sleeves, and a showy wide-brimmed hat. (Dolly Varden was the smartly dressed character in Charles Dickens' novel *Barnaby Rudge.*)

Late-nineteenth-century Scottish Celts

Left: The woman wears a suit of bold plaid that features a two-tier shoulder cape over a man-tailored jacket. The overskirt has a small bustle; the underskirt of the same fabric is box-pleated. She wears a rolled-brim cloth hat of the same plaid. **Center:** The boy is dressed in a brass-buttoned jacket worn over a plaid kilt, and a long fringed scarf of the same plaid is fastened at his shoulder. **Right:** The man wears a dark business suit; he has thrown a large woolen scarf over his arm and shoulder.

Early-twentieth-century national costumes

There was a movement to create a national costume in Ireland in the early part of the twentieth century; designers were asked to create a "folk" costume drawing on the Celtic traditions in Irish dress. The woman on the left wears the 1905 version of the national costume; the woman on the right wears the 1920 winning entry. The later outfit reflects the less conservative styles of the 1920s. Both utilize the geometric patterns representative of Irish illuminated manuscripts such as the early-ninth-century Book of Kells.

Late-twentieth-century Irish step dancers

The two most favored costumes for step dancing are the jacketed kilt and the fitted princess-style dress. Brats (short capes) are worn with both styles. The boy, at the left, wears a plain shoulder brat, while the girl on the right has an elaborately embroidered multi-colored brat in a modern Celtic design. The dancer in the center wears the princess style, with flared skirt and white eyelet cuffs and collar. She dances in ghillies, traditional Celtic footwear. The wool costume is embroidered in multicolored silk thread in an abstract Celtic pattern.

Celtic headgear, weapons, and jewelry

a. Roman era Teutonic Celt, 100 B.C. **b.** Roman era Gallic-Celtic warrior, A.D. 100. **c.** Roman era Gallic-Celtic chieftain, A.D. 100. **d.** Roman era Gallic-Celt. **e.** 3rd cent. B.C. **f.** fibula. **g.** Roman era Teutonic-Celtic. **h.** Roman era Teutonic-Celt. **i.** Roman era upswept hairstyle. **j.** Teutonic Celt, A.D. 100. **k.** torque neck ornament. **l.** Teutonic-Celtic helmet, 150 B.C. **m.** Arthurian era, A.D. 500. **n.** Arthurian era, A.D. 500. **o.** Arthurian era, A.D. 500. **p.** "Wilde Irish" Celt, 15th-16th cent. **q.** Arthurian era, A.D. 500. **r.** ax blade. **s.** dagger. **t.** Irish Celt, 16th cent. **u.** Irish Celt, 16th cent. **v.** Irish Celt, 16th cent.

Celtic headgear, footwear, weapons, jewelry, and accessories

a. 19th cent. **b.** 19th cent. **c.** boy's cap, 19th–20th cent. **d.** Scottish, 19th cent. **e.** fisherman, 19th–20th cent. **f.** 19th–20th cent. **g.** brooch. **h.** 19th cent. **i.** fibula. **j.** Breton-Celtic headdress, 19th–20th cent. **k.** ghillie, 100 B.C.–A.D. 100. **l.** A.D. 700. **m.** 17th cent. **n.** child's boot, 17th cent. **o.** patten, 17th cent. **p.** 16th cent. **q.** sporran, 17th cent. **r.** pre-historic jet necklace. **s.** earrings, 1,200 B.C. **t.** brooch. **u.** cuarans, 18th cent. **v.** fibulae, 7th cent. **w.** top and bottom: battle axes; center: cudgel, 12th cent. B.C.